Contents

		page
The Gurus in this Book		vii
Introduction		ix
Chapter 1	Welcome to the Machine	1
Chapter 2	The Company Man	17
Chapter 3	To Create a Customer	31
Chapter 4	The Management Superstar	46
Chapter 5	The Best of the Rest	55
Activities		61

Contents

Management Gurus

DAVID EVANS

Level 4

Consultant Editor: David Evans
Series Editors: Andy Hopkins and Jocelyn Potter

Pearson Education Limited
Edinburgh Gate, Harlow,
Essex CM20 2JE, England
and Associated Companies throughout the world.

ISBN 0 582 43046 1

First published 2000

3 5 7 9 10 8 6 4

Copyright © David Evans 2000

Typeset by Ferdinand Pageworks, London
Set in 11/14pt Bembo .
Printed in Spain by Mateu Cromo, S.A. Pinto (Madrid)

Published by Pearson Education Limited in association with
Penguin Books Ltd, both companies being subsidiaries of Pearson Plc

Acknowledgements:
The Ronald Grant Archive: p. 1; Corbis: pp. 5, 18, 32 and 47;
Quadrant Picture Library: p. 14; Images Colour Library: p. 29;
Popperfoto: p. 44; Elizabeth Handy: p. 57

For a complete list of titles available in the Penguin Readers series please write to your local
Pearson Education office or contact: Penguin Readers Marketing Department,
Pearson Education, Edinburgh Gate, Harlow, Essex, CM20 2JE.

Business Wordlist

accountant a person who reports the financial health of a business

branch a part of a large organization, often a shop or an office

capital money that helps to build a new business

compete to try to win

consultant a person who gives business advice

contract a formal legal agreement

corporation a big company

deal to buy and sell

expand to increase or grow

finances the amount of money that a business or person has

industry a type of business

loss the amount of money that a business loses

negotiate to try to come to an agreement with another person

objective a business aim

partnership a business that is owned by two or more people

profit money that is made in business

risk the danger of losing money

sack to tell someone to leave their job

share a piece of paper that says that you own a part of a company

stock exchange a place where people buy and sell shares

The Gurus in this Book

Frederick Taylor (1856–1917) the man who believed that management was a science. For most of the last century almost every business person believed him.

Alfred P. Sloan (1875–1966) the man who made General Motors the biggest, richest and most powerful company of all time. How did he do it?

Peter Drucker (1909–) the man who invented modern management and saw all the changes of the modern world many years before they happened.

Tom Peters (1942–) the pop star of the management world. You either hate him or you love him, but you have to listen to what he says.

Rosabeth Moss Kanter (1943–) the woman who said that business was competing in a company Olympics. So what does a company need to do to succeed?

Charles Handy (1932–) the man who suggests that 'upside down' thinking is the solution to the problems of the modern business world. But what exactly does he mean?

Management Gurus is for people who want to find out about why the modern business world works like it does!

Introduction

'I know nothing. In this world we all know nothing. Zero. And do you know why? It's because the business world is changing too quickly.' . . .

A few people now start to laugh. So the man on the stage stops and points at them.

'Why are you laughing? General Motors was the biggest company in the world. It was probably a hundred times bigger than your company. And its managers were probably a hundred times better too. But their problem was that they thought they knew it all and, really, they knew nothing. And that is my message today.'

The people who are watching this man are all very successful businessmen and businesswomen. So why are they watching a man who knows nothing? Why do they listen to his insults? The answer is because the man is a management guru.

'Guru' is an Indian word for a religious teacher. A guru is a person who thinks deeply about life. In India, they are admired and loved by society because they are wise and full of ideas. But in the USA and Europe, the word has a slightly different meaning. It is a word that often describes people who write and talk about business and management. These gurus are not trying to answer questions like, 'How can we live in peace?' and 'What is the meaning of life?' Instead, they ask, 'How can I make more profit?' and 'Why don't people work harder?'

In recent years, the ideas of the management gurus have had a big effect not just on business, but also on politics, schools, hospitals and everyday life styles.

This book introduces six management gurus whose thinking has created the modern business world, even though they might say they know nothing!

Chapter 1 Welcome to the Machine

Frederick Taylor

In his film of 1936, *Modern Times,* Charlie Chaplin shows business life as a kind of bad dream. The film is set in a huge factory where people are simply parts of a machine. The workers are not allowed to talk and they are not expected to think. Their jobs are boring and their lives are ruled by the clock. Every action is measured by managers in white coats. Above them all, there is the figure of the boss. He's the man who owns everything, controls everything and sees everything. He even gives orders to workers while they're in the company's washrooms!

Charlie Chaplin in Modern Times.

According to Chaplin, this was the terrible world that had been created by the ideas of Frederick Taylor. Today, Taylor is remembered as the father of scientific management. He has almost certainly had a bigger effect on business than any other thinker. His methods were copied by businessmen like Henry Ford in the USA and political leaders like Lenin in Russia. Even now, many companies are still managed according to his ideas.

But there has always been one big problem with Frederick Taylor and his ideas. He never really understood people. In his business life, he was never a very successful manager because he was always arguing with his workers. In his private life he often behaved in a very strange way.

In fact, in his later years, he met one of his old bosses, Charles Harrah, at the entrance to a hotel.

'How are you?' asked Taylor.

'Oh, very well,' said Harrah, 'I'm making millions and millions of dollars. In fact, I'm planning to build a hospital for mad people.'

'Oh really?' said Taylor.

'Yes, really,' said Harrah, 'and I'm saving a whole floor of it for you.'

♦

Frederick Taylor never intended to go into management. His family was one of the richest in Philadelphia and his parents had great hopes for him. The Taylors lived in a large house with servants. They took expensive holidays in Europe and by the age of sixteen, young Fred had learnt both French and German. It seemed he was certain to live the life of a rich gentleman.

At school, Fred was an excellent student and a fine sportsman, who loved tennis. When the USA's top university, Harvard, accepted him as a law student, it seemed that his future was decided. But Frederick Taylor had one big problem; he always tried too hard at everything. To pass Harvard's entrance examination, he had studied night and day and had read too many books. Soon after Harvard accepted him, he found that he had a serious problem with his eyes.

He was very worried and said to his parents, 'If I have problems with my eyes now, what will they be like after several more years of hard study?'

His parents tried to make him feel better.

'They'll get better, Fred,' they told him. 'You just need some rest.'

But rest was something that Taylor never wanted. He didn't wait for his eyes to improve; instead, he changed the direction of his life completely. His parents were shocked when he told them about his plans.

'How can you do this,' they asked him, 'after the education that you've had?'

But Taylor knew what he wanted.

'I've decided to take a job as an ordinary worker in one of our local factories.'

Taylor had always hated working with his hands, but for the next four years, he learnt to cut metal and to operate machines. His colleagues were rough men from the poor parts of Pittsburgh. They were surprised to find this young gentleman in their factory and wondered why he was there. Taylor was clearly very different from them. He was a religious young man and he didn't like the way they drank alcohol or smoked tobacco. But his colleagues were friendly to Taylor and he was soon surprising other members of his family with the bad language that he had learnt at his workplace.

But Taylor was not a great success at the factory, and when his training was finished, his boss told him that there was no future for him there. At the age of twenty-two, Taylor found that he was unemployed. What could he do? He didn't want to ask for help from his rich friends and he didn't want to use his family money to make a new start. Instead, once again, he chose the most difficult direction. He took a job as an ordinary worker at another Pittsburgh factory – the Midvale Steel Works.

◆

Midvale was a group of five or six old buildings in the dirtiest part of the city. Thick black smoke poured from its chimneys into the sky. The workers were rougher than at his last job and the bosses were tougher. But Taylor knew that he could succeed.

His experience over the past few years had made him interested in machines. When Midvale's owner, William Sellars, asked some of the workers for their opinion of his plans for a new machine, Taylor saw a great opportunity. He took Sellars's plans home and studied them carefully. He immediately noticed a few problems and over the next few days, he worked late into the night to find some solutions to them.

At the start of the next week, he knocked on William Sellars's door.

'What do you want?' shouted Sellars, when he saw the young worker.

'I want to talk to you about your plans for the new machine,' said Taylor. 'I've found one or two problems, I'm afraid, sir.'

'Oh, have you?' said Sellars.

'Yes, sir,' said Taylor. 'I hope you don't mind, but I've drawn some of my own ideas. I think they'll solve the problem.'

'Give them to me,' ordered Sellars.

Nervously, Taylor gave him his papers. They were the product of several nights of long, hard work.

'Taylor,' said Sellars. 'I believe that I asked you for your opinion of the new machine. Is that right?'

'Yes, sir,' said Taylor.

'And when I ask for your opinion,' continued Sellars, 'I expect your opinion. I do not expect your ideas.'

Frederick Taylor

Sellars turned away for a moment and threw Taylor's papers on to the fire in the corner of the room.

'Do you understand?' asked Sellars.

'Yes, sir,' said Taylor, as his ideas disappeared in smoke up the office chimney.

The bosses at Midvale were certainly tough with Taylor, but they could also see that he was too intelligent to stay in the same job for long. After a few months, they asked him to become the manager of a small group of workers. Taylor was excited. He thought that the workers at Midvale were lazy and he was sure that he could make them work harder.

The workers were immediately worried by him.

'You don't expect us to work harder or produce more, do you?' they asked.

'Of course, I do,' he replied. 'But don't worry, I've got a few ideas to help you. We're going to start to work scientifically.'

For the next three years at Midvale, Taylor and his workers were at war.

Taylor believed he could find the best possible way of doing every job in the factory. So he studied each worker's job until he had found a way of doing it more quickly. Then he taught the new way of working to one of the workers in his team. Taylor was a good teacher and the worker was soon working more quickly than before. Unfortunately, the other members of the team didn't like it. They felt that it made the rest of them look bad. Before long, Taylor found that every member of his team was working at the same slow speed as before. This made him very angry.

'You're here to work!' he shouted at the men. 'If you work harder, the company will make more money. If the company makes more money, you'll make more money. When you work harder, it helps everyone. Don't you understand?'

But the workers didn't understand and Taylor had to try

tougher methods. Now, when he taught a worker a new way of working, he made it completely clear that the worker had to work more quickly. If he didn't work more quickly, Taylor sacked him.

But, of course, each time a worker was sacked, it made the situation even worse. And it wasn't long before the workers took more serious action. They started breaking the factory's machines. Taylor's bosses were frightened and they asked him to solve the problem immediately. His solution was simple. Each time a machine was damaged, the workers had to pay for it.

The damage to the machines soon stopped, but Taylor's methods didn't. On one occasion, he noticed a very small mark on one of the workers' machines.

'You'll pay for this,' he said to the worker who operated it.

'But I didn't do it,' said the worker. 'That mark has always been there.'

'Don't give me excuses,' said Taylor. 'You'll pay for it.'

The workers in Taylor's team started to produce more, but his attitude was causing serious problems and his friends started worrying.

'I don't think it's safe for you to walk home at night alone,' said one of his colleagues. 'People are saying that some of the workers are planning to shoot you.'

Frederick Taylor laughed.

'Let them try,' he said.

◆

Although the Midvale workers weren't happy with his methods, Taylor was becoming more and more interested in scientific solutions to problems. His eyes were now better and so he decided to return to his studies. But this time he didn't want to study law at Harvard; instead, he wanted to become an engineer. He started a course at the Stevens Institute of Technology, a local university. The course was hard and it meant that Taylor had to study for three or four hours in the evening after a long working day at Midvale.

As Taylor learnt more about his subject, he thought of ways of using engineering ideas in other areas of life. One of these was tennis.

Because Taylor's family was so religious, he wasn't allowed to work on Sundays. But they didn't mind if he played tennis. So every Sunday, Taylor and his friend, Clarence Clark, practised tennis for hours and hours and hours. In 1881, they decided to enter the US national tennis competition – the event that is now called the US Open. Taylor knew that he and his friend were good players, but he wanted to prepare for the competition in a modern, scientific way.

Taylor realized that a good tennis player needed to be fit. But how could he get fit, when he spent so much time working and studying? Taylor's solution was simply to reduce his amount of sleep. So, after finishing his studies just after midnight every day, Taylor put on his running shoes and ran for several kilometres through the dark empty streets of Philadelphia. At first, the local police often stopped him and asked him questions. But soon they just shook their heads and said, 'It's that strange young Mr Taylor again.'

Taylor also thought hard about the tennis equipment that he was using. He was sure that he could find a way of improving it. During their Sunday practice-games, Taylor and Clark tested several new ideas.

When they arrived at the national tennis competition, people were immediately interested in them. One of the other players pointed at the unusual thing in Taylor's hand.

'You're not going to play tennis with that, are you?' he asked.

'Of course,' replied Taylor. 'Why not?'

'But it looks like a spoon,' said the young man. Everybody laughed.

'Just wait and see,' said Taylor calmly.

By the end of the competition, the laughing had stopped. Although their equipment was strange, Taylor and Clark didn't lose a game and became winners of the US national tennis competition of 1881.

◆

Back at the Midvale Steel Works, the bosses were starting to notice young Frederick Taylor. They admired his energy and his tough attitude to the workers. They also liked his ideas for new tools and machines. Certainly, nobody threw his plans on the fire any more! Soon after he finished his course in engineering in 1883, Taylor was made Midvale's Chief Engineering Officer. In just six years he had gone from the job of an ordinary worker to become one of the company's top managers.

People outside Midvale were also beginning to hear about Frederick Taylor. In 1890, he was asked to become General Manager of the Manufacturing Investment Company, a business that owned a number of paper factories. Taylor was very pleased. It was a better job and it paid more money. More importantly, it also gave him more opportunities to test his ideas about engineering and management.

But the Manufacturing Investment Company was not really ready for Taylor's ideas and he was soon having problems with both the bosses and the workers.

The owners of the company were worried about the large amounts of money that he started to spend on new machines and new equipment.

'The business can't afford this,' they told him. 'We need to make the money before we can spend it.'

But, as always, Taylor had a scientific reason for the spending.

'Each worker,' he explained, 'is worth $3,000. So if a machine can replace a worker and it costs less than $3,000, it makes perfect economic sense to buy it.'

But the owners of the company didn't agree.

The workers at the company's factories were also soon angry with Taylor. To make the company's factories safer, Taylor told some of the workers that they had to work behind bars.

'You must understand,' explained Taylor, 'that this is in your interests. I want you to be safe at work.'

But the workers didn't see things like that.

'We can't work behind bars,' they complained. 'What does he think we are? Animals? It's like working in a zoo.'

Taylor felt that everyone was criticizing him and he became more and more unhappy in his job. To make things worse, the company was not making a lot of money. Everyone agreed that Taylor had lots of ideas, but did they work? The answer seemed to be, 'No'.

Taylor didn't know what to do. Should he stay or should he go? In the end, he didn't have to make a decision.

In 1893, the US economy hit some serious problems. Suddenly, nobody had any money. People stopped buying things. The value of the US dollar dropped like a stone. It was clear that the Manufacturing Investment Company could never be a success. Taylor had to leave and find a future somewhere else.

The next few years were difficult for him. Although he tried very hard, he couldn't find a regular job. Instead, he sold advice about engineering and management to a number of companies in the north-east of the USA. It was a job that allowed Taylor to see how other companies operated. The more he saw, the more ideas he had. Now, he just needed a chance to test them.

♦

His opportunity came in 1898 when he was offered a job as manager of the Bethlehem Steel Works. Taylor couldn't wait to start work. For his first test, he chose the simplest of all the jobs in the factory. This was the job of moving pieces of iron from one place to another. For weeks, Taylor and his assistants studied the workers. They found out the best way to pick up a piece of iron. They used watches to find out how quickly a worker could carry a piece of iron over a certain distance. They also decided how much rest a worker needed in order to work as hard as possible. They tried to answer the question: what happens if we manage a human being in the same way that we operate a machine?

When their study was finished, Taylor sat down with his assistants and explained his findings.

'According to our study,' said Taylor, 'a good worker can move between forty-seven and forty-eight tons of iron a day.'

'But that's strange,' said one of the assistants. 'At the moment they only move twelve tons a day.'

'Exactly,' said Taylor. 'Isn't it great? We have a chance to show everyone that scientific management really produces results.'

'But how will we make these people work in our new way?' asked another assistant.

'No problem,' said Taylor. 'The harder they work, the more they'll earn. The company will be happy and the worker will be happy. No one can lose!'

Next they needed a worker to test the results of the study. Taylor's assistants now knew all the workers very well and they immediately suggested a young man called Schmidt. He was big and strong and he had a young family, so it was certain that he needed more money.

At the factory one day, Taylor called Schmidt to him.

'Schmidt,' said Taylor. 'Are you an expensive man or a cheap man?'

Schmidt looked at him and thought hard.

'What do you mean?' he asked.

'Oh, really, Mr Schmidt,' said Taylor, 'it's not a very difficult question. Let me say it another way. Would you prefer to earn $1.15 an hour or $1.85?'

Schmidt still seemed uncertain, so Taylor continued, 'I think, Mr Schmidt, that you'd prefer to earn $1.85. Everyone prefers to earn more for their time. It's a law of human nature.'

'Maybe,' agreed Schmidt.

'Excellent,' said Taylor. 'Now, if you want to earn $1.85, you must do exactly as I tell you. When I tell you to pick up a piece of iron, you pick it up. When I tell you to walk, you walk. And when I tell you to rest, you rest. Do you agree?'

The other workers were shaking their heads.

'Don't listen to him,' they called to their colleague. But Schmidt was already thinking of the extra money.

'OK,' he said. 'I'll do it.'

Schmidt did exactly as he was told and he was soon moving 60 per cent more iron every day. The extra money that he earned made a big difference to his life. The other workers didn't like Taylor's ideas, but they also didn't like the fact that Schmidt was earning much more money than them. One by one, they agreed to use Taylor's new method of working.

But many of the workers found that they couldn't earn as much as Schmidt, simply because they weren't as strong as him. In fact, seven out of eight workers couldn't work as hard as Taylor asked. Taylor saw only one solution; they had to leave.

Some of the other managers at the company started to worry.

'Are you sure your new method is fair?' they asked him.

'Of course, it is,' replied Taylor. 'These men do an honest day's work for an honest day's pay. Of course, it's sad that some people have to leave. But one of the most important things about good management is finding the right man for the right job.'

Taylor soon started to organize the work of the rest of the factory in the same way. First, he watched the workers and measured the speed of every move they made. Then he decided on the quickest way of doing each job and taught that method to the workers. Finally, he chose the best workers for every job and told the others to find work somewhere else. Again, the results were excellent.

But Taylor's attitude was making him more and more enemies at Bethlehem. The workers liked earning more money, but they hated Taylor's methods. The company's owners weren't sure of him, especially because he was again spending large amounts of money on new equipment. In May 1901, he was sacked. Although Taylor was only forty-five, it was the last manager's job that he had in his life.

◆

Taylor had had enough of business. But at least he had shown that his idea of scientific management could work. He went back to his house in the country and wrote pieces for magazines and newspapers that explained his ideas. He travelled round the country and gave talks to groups of businessmen and engineers. Slowly, more and more people became interested in the idea of scientific management.

Then, in 1910, Taylor suddenly became famous. The US government was having a meeting about the different costs of train and sea travel. The railway companies said they needed more money from taxes. The shipowners said that they didn't. To support their argument, the shipowners explained that the railway companies wouldn't need the money if they improved their management. To explain their point they asked some managers to talk about a man called Frederick Taylor and a new idea called scientific management.

'If the railways introduce this idea,' one manager told the US government, 'they will save a million dollars a day.'

Another manager said that scientific management could cut costs and increase workers' pay by 100 per cent.

The next day, Taylor's name and a description of his ideas were in all the newspapers. Everybody in the US business world was talking about scientific management.

In fact, the time was just right for Taylor's ideas. In the early 1900s in Detroit, another engineer, called Henry Ford, had started a new business that made cars. At that time, cars were very expensive and were only owned by the richest people in the world. But Ford believed that it was possible to sell cars at a price that ordinary people could afford. He simply needed to reduce the cost of making them. To do this, he decided to make just one kind of car in just one colour – the famous black Model T Ford. At his factory, he also started making Model Ts in a new way. His method was to move the car along a line while workers added pieces to it. The workers' jobs were very boring, because they just did the same thing again and again and again, all day long. But

The famous black Model T Ford.

Ford wasn't worried about that; for him workers were just another part of the machine. He once said, 'When I want a pair of hands, why do I get a human being as well?'

The Ford Motor Company was very successful. Its factory in Detroit produced a new car every forty seconds, and the price of a new Ford car soon fell below $300. As a result, millions of people bought Ford cars and Henry Ford became the richest man in the world.

Of course, everybody wanted to know the secrets of his success. When they heard about Frederick Taylor, many believed that he could give them the answers they wanted. The ideas of Ford and Taylor were very similar. Both Ford and Taylor believed that workers didn't want or need to have responsibility. Without their managers, workers were nothing. It was the manager's job to find the best workers and to teach them to work in the best possible way. It didn't matter if the workers were unhappy. They were paid an honest day's pay for an honest day's work and it was their job simply to obey.

These were the ideas that Taylor wrote about in his book of 1911, *The Principles of Scientific Management*. It was a huge success. When he gave a talk in New York City some time later, it was attended by 69,000 people!

◆

Managers who followed Taylor's ideas were famous for their watches. They all wanted people to work as quickly as possible, so they needed their watches to measure the workers' speed. Taylor, too, loved watches and carried an expensive Swiss one with him wherever he went. In 1917, when he was taken into hospital because of an illness, the doctors and nurses soon noticed that Taylor always wound his watch at exactly the same time every day. Then early one morning, a nurse heard a sound from Taylor's room at four o'clock in the morning.

15

'How strange,' she thought. 'Mr Taylor usually has such regular habits. Why is he winding his watch so early in the day?'

In fact, it was Taylor's last action. When the nurse looked into the room just an hour later, she found that Taylor was dead. In a way it seemed right that this was the final action of the man who had made so many others servants of the clock.

◆

In the years after his death, the ideas of Frederick Taylor spread around the world. His books were translated into many different languages. Factories from California to Siberia were organized according to his methods. Machines came first and people came second. Managers learnt to control and workers were taught to obey. The boss's word was law.

But today, many people question Frederick Taylor's scientific management. Does it really produce the best results? Do managers always know best? Is it true that people only work for money? Is it true that they don't want responsibility?

But although his ideas are often questioned, it's certain that there are many businesses in the world today that still haven't forgotten the lessons of Frederick Taylor.

Chapter 2   The Company Man

Alfred P. Sloan

If it's good for America it's good for General Motors and if it's good for General Motors it's good for America.

Charles E. Wilson

Is a company as important as a country? Are the interests of a business the same as the interests of a nation? Most people would answer 'no' to both questions. But when you're talking about General Motors you can't be so sure.

Certainly, when the General Motors manager, Charles E. Wilson, said those words at a meeting with the US government in the early 1950s, nobody was surprised. At the time, General Motors was the biggest company in the world – it employed more than 750,000 people. It made some of the most famous products in the world – cars with names like Chevrolet, Cadillac and Buick. It was also the richest company in the world and it sometimes made profits of over $2 billion. But perhaps most important of all, General Motors' boss, Alfred P. Sloan, was the most admired businessman of the last century.

Sloan was admired because his ideas were copied by every other big business in the middle years of the twentieth century. He was admired because he had created a company that was bigger and more powerful than many small, rich countries. But his colleagues knew the real reason for Sloan's success; he was a man who always put business first.

Sloan had no children and no interests outside work. He rarely saw his wife because he often slept in a small bed at the General

17

Alfred P. Sloan

Motors offices. In fact, he took his job so seriously that he didn't even allow himself to have any friends.

'Some people like to be alone,' he once said. 'I don't. But I have a duty not to have friends in the workplace.'

◆

Sloan became the boss of General Motors in the early 1920s, at a time when the company was having serious problems. GM had been started by the US businessman, Billy Durant. Durant collected companies like some people collect stamps. He owned companies that made everything from cars to fridges. He thought that if he owned enough companies, one or two of them were certain to be successful. Unfortunately he was wrong. Because although he was good at buying companies, he was useless at managing them. In fact, Durant was such a difficult man that he lost all his best employees, including some of the most famous names in the car business. Walter Chrysler worked for Durant for a time, but he soon left and started the successful Chrysler Corporation. Another employee was sacked because he smoked a cigarette in Durant's office. His name was Louis Chevrolet.

By 1920, General Motors was in a mess. It employed too many people, it had too many managers, it made too many kinds of cars and it was losing lots of money. Even Billy Durant realized that it couldn't continue. So he sold GM to one of the great names of early US business, Pierre du Pont. Du Pont could see that GM showed promise, but it needed a good manager. So du Pont turned to Alfred Sloan.

At the time, Sloan was forty-three years old and he was already a great success. He had started twenty years before, when he borrowed $5,000 from his father and bought a company called Hyatt. Hyatt did not look like a very good business. It made small metal balls that were used in trains and other vehicles and it was making no more than $2,000 a month. But Sloan was confident

19

that he could turn Hyatt into a success. He believed that the new car business presented a great opportunity for his company's products. So he talked to all the important people in the USA's car business and learnt as much as possible about making cars. Before long Hyatt was making profits of over $4 million a year.

When Sloan arrived at General Motors, he saw immediately that he needed to organize the company in a new way. At that time, General Motors was producing eight different cars but had only 12 per cent of the car market. By comparison, Ford produced one car – the Model T – and had over 60 per cent of the market. What could Sloan do?

Perhaps GM should simply copy Ford's idea and cut its number of cars from eight to one. But Sloan had different ideas. He thought that customers were getting tired of Ford's Model T. Of course, they liked it because it was cheap and because it worked well. But customers wanted more choice. Ford advertised its Model T by saying, 'You can have any colour you want, but it has to be black.'

It was a good joke, but it was also true. Sloan realized that he could win customers if he offered something different. So he thought carefully about GM's position in the market and prepared his ideas.

Although he was not an old man, Sloan was already suffering from hearing problems. For that reason, he always used a hearing aid in meetings. When he wanted to listen, he switched it on; before he spoke, he always switched it off. It was once described as the greatest management tool in history. At the meeting to decide GM's future direction, he listened carefully to the ideas of his colleagues.

'We need to learn the lessons of Mr Ford,' said one manager. 'We must learn to produce our cars as quickly and as cheaply as possible. That's the only way to succeed in this business.'

'I don't agree,' said another manager. 'We have a choice. There are two main markets for cars in this country. We can sell expensive upmarket cars to people who have good taste and plenty of money, or we can sell cheap downmarket cars to people who have neither.'

Everyone in the room laughed.

When Sloan had heard all the managers' ideas, he switched off his hearing aid with a loud noise. The managers all turned towards him and waited for him to speak.

'Thank you for your ideas, gentlemen,' said Sloan. 'But I must disagree with you. Our company has more choices than you have described. I believe that General Motors should sell a car for every pocket and every purpose.'

The managers looked at each other.

'Let me explain what I mean,' continued Sloan. 'We own a number of companies at the moment. The problem is that they are all fighting in the same market. First, I suggest that we reduce our number of companies to five. Second, I suggest that each of these companies sells its cars to a different part of the market. For example, Cadillac could sell its cars to the rich people with good taste that you talked about earlier. We could sell Buicks to younger people with a little less money. Oldsmobile could be sold to richer families; Pontiac to poorer ones. Chevrolet, perhaps, could sell its cars to the working man. Do you follow my thinking?'

One of the managers held up a finger to show that he wanted to ask a question. Sloan switched on his hearing aid again.

'How does this affect the organization of the company?' the manager asked.

There was another noise from the hearing aid.

'That,' said Sloan, 'is a very good question. You see, gentlemen, I want an organization with five different companies selling cars to five different markets. I'm sure there will sometimes be competition between these five companies. If that happens that's fine with me. But General Motors doesn't just need competition. The company must also understand where it's going. There must be some central control. That's why I am here. We must have a clear direction and we must also have central financial control. If we can do this, then I am sure that General Motors will have a great future.'

Sloan was right. The careful mix between central control and competition produced a company that could compete with Ford and even beat it. While Ford continued to build the same old black Model T, GM produced new cars and new ideas all the time. Customers were offered not just a choice of five different cars, but a choice of colours, too. Every year, GM produced cars with a few small differences, so that people didn't keep the same car for years and years; instead, they always wanted to buy the latest model. Just three years after Alfred Sloan's appointment, General Motors left Ford behind and became the USA's biggest car company.

The 1920s was a good time for the US car business. The government built roads across the country and small businessmen built all kinds of things beside them. Before long, US roads were lined with petrol stations, cinemas, hotels and restaurants. Every American wanted to be on the road and General Motors went from one success to another. It seemed that nothing could stop the car.

But, of course, one thing can always stop a car: a crash. But the crash that stopped General Motors in 1929 wasn't a car crash; it was a financial crash.

On 24 October 1929, the prices of shares on the Wall Street Stock Exchange in New York started falling . . . and they fell . . . and fell . . . and fell. People who had been rich the day before, woke up and found that they were poor. People who had been poor the day before, found that they had nothing to eat and nowhere to live. Businesses failed. Bankers killed themselves.

Millions of workers lost their jobs. In that kind of situation, who's going to spend a lot of money on a new car?

The years that followed were tough for every business, everywhere in the world. Sales of General Motors' cars fell by 70 per cent. Sloan knew he had to make some tough decisions. But before Sloan took a decision, he believed that it was his duty to think about all possibilities. For him a manager was not just a business person who was interested only in profit. In Sloan's eyes, a manager was a professional, like a doctor or a dentist, and professionals always kept an open mind and always listened to the facts. So, even in the middle of the most difficult times, Sloan always wanted the opinions of his managers.

In 1932, GM's Cadillac company was having real problems. Cadillacs were very expensive cars and the crash of the American economy had hit their sales especially hard. Cadillac was losing large amounts of money. At the meeting to decide Cadillac's future, Sloan and all his managers had reached agreement.

'The facts in this case are quite clear,' said Sloan. 'Cadillac must be closed. So, now our only decision is – do we keep the Cadillac name and put it on another car or do we just forget about it?'

At that moment, there was a knock on the door and one of Cadillac's young middle managers, Nick Dreystadt, walked into the room. Dreystadt was an untidy man who spoke with a strong German accent. Nervously, he looked around at Sloan and the other top GM managers.

'I'm sorry to interrupt,' said Dreystadt, 'but I know that you are thinking of closing Cadillac. Before you take any decision, I'd like you to listen to my plan. With this plan, I am sure that Cadillac will be back in profit within eighteen months.'

Several of the top managers were very angry with Dreystadt. How did this middle manager dare to interrupt their meeting with his ideas? But Alfred Sloan stayed calm and polite.

'Please continue, Mr Dreystadt,' he said.

'Well,' said Dreystadt, 'I have noticed that Cadillacs are the most popular car with rich black people.'

'What do you mean?' said one of the top managers. 'That's impossible. We don't sell Cadillacs to black people. It's against our rules.'

'I know,' said Dreystadt, 'but rich black people are paying white people to buy Cadillacs for them.'

'I don't understand,' said the manager, 'why are they doing this?'

'Well,' continued Dreystadt, 'as we all know it's difficult for black people to do many things in the USA. Rich black people are not allowed to buy expensive houses in the areas where rich white people live. But, of course, if you're a successful black doctor, or a black businessman, or a black sportsman, you still want to show people that you're rich and successful. A Cadillac is one of the few ways that these people can do this.'

'Very interesting, Mr Dreystadt,' said Alfred Sloan. 'So what exactly are you suggesting?'

'I want us to change our ideas about Cadillac. We shouldn't stop black people from buying them. Instead, they should be our main market.'

Alfred Sloan and the other top managers discussed Dreystadt's idea for a few minutes and then Alfred Sloan switched off his hearing aid and looked at Dreystadt.

'OK, Mr Dreystadt,' said Sloan. 'We'd like to go ahead with your idea. We won't close Cadillac. Not yet, at least.'

Dreystadt thanked Sloan. He was just leaving the room, when one of GM's top managers spoke to him: 'You realize that if you fail, there won't be a job for you at GM, don't you?'

'Of course, I do,' replied Dreystadt.

'But I don't,' interrupted Alfred Sloan quickly. 'If you fail, Mr Dreystadt, there won't be a job for you at Cadillac. There won't be a Cadillac. But as long as there is a General Motors and as long as I run it, there will always be a job for a man who takes responsibility. There will always be a job for a man who has the right attitude and imagination.'

Alfred Sloan looked calmly at Dreystadt.

'Mr Dreystadt, you worry about the future of Cadillac. I'll worry about your future at General Motors.'

Dreystadt and Sloan didn't need to worry. Thanks to Dreystadt's plan Cadillac stopped losing money within a year and it was soon making a healthy profit.

It was often difficult for Sloan to mix central control and competition. GM expected its managers to be company men (at that time it didn't have women managers). Managers were all expected to wear dark suits and light shirts. Their offices on the fourteenth floor of the main General Motors building were all decorated in the same way. They were expected to have similar values and similar attitudes. This sometimes made it difficult for GM's managers to have a discussion. Before Sloan took a decision, he always wanted to hear opinions from all parts of his huge company. But on one occasion a manager presented such an excellent plan at a meeting that everyone immediately agreed with it. This didn't please Sloan at all. He switched off his hearing aid and looked round the room.

'So, gentlemen,' he said, 'we're all in complete agreement, are we?'

The managers at the meeting all smiled.

'In that case,' Sloan continued, 'I suggest that we delay our decision on this plan. Let's meet again when we've had a chance to think about it. Before we take any big decision, I expect at least some disagreement.'

Managers at General Motors had a good life. Of course, they worked very hard and they were always under lots of pressure. But they were always well paid. In fact, some of them even earned more than Sloan himself. He believed that ability should be rewarded.

But his attitude to GM's workers was very different. GM workers earned good money when the company was producing lots of cars. But in the bad times, there was no job for them and they earned nothing at all. Their organization, the United Automobile Workers, often tried to discuss the workers' conditions with the GM management, but Sloan refused to speak to them.

The early years of the 1930s were bad for the company, but they were even worse for the workers and their families. By the winter of 1936, they had had enough. As the company was preparing its new cars for 1937, the workers at the company's main factory in the town of Flint stopped working, and sat down. Their unemployed colleagues from outside joined them and sat down in the factory as well. Sloan and the GM managers were very angry and asked the local police for help. But the police were not interested and the 'sit-down strike' continued through Christmas and into the next year. By February, the company's car production had fallen to almost zero, while GM's competitors Ford and Chrysler were producing more and more cars to make the most of the opportunity. In the end, Sloan and his managers had to accept the situation and they agreed to start talks with the United Automobile Workers about conditions in their factories. It was one of the few times that Sloan lost a fight.

The lives of GM's workers improved slightly after that, but things didn't really change at General Motors until December 1941. That was when Japanese planes bombed US warships at Pearl Harbour in Hawaii and the USA entered the Second World War. For the next few years, GM had to forget about its normal business. Many of its workers and managers became soldiers, while its factories produced equipment for the US war machine.

When the war finished in 1946, Sloan had to prepare for a

completely new age of US business. Every boss in the USA was thinking hard about his own business and his plans for it. But Sloan had other worries too. He was already looking a long way into the future. And when he looked into the future, he wasn't worried about GM; he was worried about its great competitor, Ford.

Henry Ford's ideas had worked very well in the early days of his company, but he had refused to move with the times. His Model T car had been such a success that he didn't want to change it in any way. In fact, when one of his engineers showed him an improved model, Henry Ford kicked it until it fell to pieces! So in the years before the war, while GM was changing its cars every year, Ford was falling further and further behind.

Henry Ford's ideas about management had also created problems. While Sloan was building an organization which accepted competition, Henry Ford was trying to increase his central control. Ford had spies everywhere in the company who told him about any new ideas or plans. The result was that his managers were afraid of taking any decisions.

Nothing really changed when Henry Ford's son, Edsel, replaced him as boss of the company and when Edsel died in 1944, the Ford Motor Company was in serious trouble. Its next boss was Henry Ford's grandson, Henry Ford II. He was just twenty-six years old and had no experience of the car business. He hadn't even finished his university education.

For General Motors it seemed like a great opportunity. It was a chance for them to finish their biggest competitor. But Alfred Sloan didn't see it that way.

'A successful business needs strong competition,' he said. He was also worried about the US government. What would it do if GM became too big and too powerful? Sloan decided, secretly, to help Henry Ford II whenever he could. He even arranged for him to employ some of GM's best managers.

Ford was soon a strong company again and, as Alfred Sloan had thought, GM grew stronger because of the competition. The years after the war were great times for the US car business.

In the 1920s Sloan had said that GM should make changes to its cars every year. He wanted people to buy a new car not because it didn't work any more, but because it had gone out of fashion. The result was that GM added more and more new details to its cars and they started to look stranger and stranger.

In the 1940s and 1950s, the person responsible for the look of GM's cars was a man called Harley Earl. He had started his working life in Los Angeles, where he created cars for Hollywood films. When he moved to General Motors, he brought his showbusiness attitude with him. While most managers at General Motors wore a white shirt and a blue suit, Earl always arrived at the office in a white suit and a blue shirt. His ideas for GM's cars were just as crazy.

Earl wasn't worried about safety or speed, he only cared about style. GM's cars got longer and lower. They also got heavier as he added more and more things, like special lights and shiny metal handles. He even copied parts of planes and spaceships and put them on to GM's new cars. By the end of the 1950s, a GM Cadillac had two large tails on the back and swept through the streets of US cities like a machine from another world.

Of course, many people criticized them. The leader of the Soviet Union, Nikita Kruschev, couldn't understand them at all.

'What do these things do?' he asked, when he saw a GM car for the first time.

US religious leaders hated them.

'Who are the madmen who build these cars?' asked one of them.

A Ford manager described a GM car of the time as 'a piece of soap with wheels on'.

A 1950s GM Cadillac.

But the American people loved them. They were the cars of the American dream. Films were made about them. Pop stars like Eddie Cochran sang songs about them. General Motors was not just the biggest, it was not just the richest, it was also the most famous company in the world.

◆

In the years to come, General Motors started to face problems. Alfred Sloan's method of organization meant that managers spent a long time in meetings and that the company often took decisions slowly. Until the end of the 1960s this hadn't been a special problem. But as the speed of business life got faster, GM sometimes found that it was too slow to solve the problems and take the opportunites of the modern world. Its huge beautiful cars were also expensive and used too much petrol. When the price of petrol rose suddenly in the early 1970s, more and more people started driving smaller cheaper cars from Japan.

But when Alfred Sloan died in 1966 that was all in the future. When people looked back on his life at that time, few could find fault with his leadership of General Motors. He had controlled the direction of the company and its finances, and he had also allowed its car companies to work as separate organizations. He had introduced the idea of the manager as a professional, like a doctor or a dentist, who puts facts before emotions when taking a decision. He had also thought about the market in a new way. Before Sloan, people thought that they simply had to sell the right product to the right people; after Sloan, people realized that a new product creates a new market.

Everyone agreed that Sloan had been the perfect company man.

Chapter 3   To Create a Customer

Peter Drucker

There is a lot of competition among the world's top management gurus. But, strangely, they all agree on the answer to the question: who is the most important modern management thinker? The answer is obviously Peter Drucker. Everyone agrees that he is the man who invented modern management. He was the first person to think carefully about the position of business in society. He supported the idea of giving more power to workers at a time when the boss's word was law. He saw the importance of computers before Bill Gates had learnt to read. He also said that government businesses should return to the private part of the economy over twenty years before the idea changed the face of Europe.

But Drucker is not just a business specialist. He has written two books of fiction and he has also taught university courses on Japanese art. Even his books about business are full of ideas and information from history and literature. 'How many Englishmen were gentlemen in the nineteenth century?' he asks in one of his books. (Not many, is his answer.) He often gives examples from the works of Jane Austen and Charles Dickens to explain his ideas about company life.

The truth is that Drucker is not a normal management writer. He has no real experience of business, because he has spent most of his life in universities. And although he has worked in the USA for over half a century, he is not really an American. Perhaps that's why he's always been a little bit different.

♦

Peter Drucker

Drucker was born in 1909 and grew up in Vienna, Austria. When he was a teenager in the 1920s, Vienna was a city that lived in the past. Just a few years before, it had been the capital of an area that stretched from the Alps to the edge of Russia. More than 50 million people lived there. Vienna's wonderful palaces had welcomed the world's richest and most powerful leaders. Its cafés had been full of great artists and writers. Its concert halls and theatres produced some of the greatest music and plays in all of Europe. But the First World War changed all that. At the end of the war, Austria found that it had lost its power, most of its land and nearly all of its people. By the early 1920s, Austria was a small country of just 6.5 million people, with no real place on the world's stage.

Certainly, Austria had changed, but its people hadn't forgotten its traditions − especially, its tradition of great work in art and science. Peter Drucker's family was typical. His grandmother was a musician who had played for Gustav Mahler; his father had been a friend of Sigmund Freud. Drucker grew up in a home where people spoke three languages. They discussed science, books and mathematics in the way that many modern families talk about TV and sport today.

◆

It was soon clear that the young Peter Drucker was very clever. He got excellent results at school and at the age of seventeen, he decided to leave Austria and find a new life. He moved to Hamburg in the north of Germany. His father wanted him to become a full-time student at Hamburg University. But the idea was too boring for Drucker.

'Students live in a dream that is two parts beer and one part sex,' he said. He wanted to find out about real life. So, he worked in an office job during the day and studied law in the university library in the evenings. His father was worried. He thought that his son was wasting his life. But Drucker soon proved him wrong.

At the age of twenty, he was already publishing his writing in important magazines. His first report was about the world economy. It was very well written and very cleverly argued; sadly, it was also very wrong.

'The world economy looks good,' he wrote. 'The New York Stock Exchange will almost certainly go up.'

The report appeared in September 1929. Just one month later, the New York Stock Exchange crashed. It was the worst financial disaster of the twentieth century. Drucker said that after that experience, he never tried to make guesses about the financial future again.

◆

The crash of the New York Stock Exchange had a terrible effect on all the economies of the world. And one of the places that suffered most was Germany. German businesses failed, the value of German money fell and millions of ordinary Germans lost their jobs. Some German families had to sell everything they owned so that they could still afford to eat. Drucker was shocked by the problems that he saw. But he was even more shocked by the events that followed.

It seemed that Germany's politicians could do nothing to help their people. Many ordinary Germans lost hope in their government and looked for other solutions to their problems. One person who said that he had the answer was Adolf Hitler. Support for Hitler grew as Germany's problems got worse. In 1932, Hitler and his Nazi party came to power.

In the early 1930s, Drucker had moved to Frankfurt and had taken a job as a journalist for a newspaper. He was in an excellent position to see the changes in German life and he was frightened by what he saw. But what should he do? Should he stay and fight the Nazis, or should he leave the country and find a new life somewhere else?

It was soon clear that he had no choice. Drucker was working on a book about a writer and thinker called Julius Stahl. He knew that Stahl's ideas were very different from the ideas of people in the Nazi party. When the book was published, he was very worried. In fact he was right to be worried. The Nazis hated the book so much that they burnt it. Drucker realized that he had to leave the country.

◆

In 1933, Drucker moved to London. There, he worked for banks or other financial organizations during the day and continued to write in the evenings. But the news from Germany got worse and worse and he became more and more worried about the political situation in Europe.

But he also had some happy times in London. One day he was on his way to catch a train at a London station when he saw a beautiful young woman on the moving stairs next to him. She was going up and he was going down. But it wasn't just that she was beautiful, he also recognized her! It was a woman he had known in Hamburg called Doris. When he got to the bottom of the moving stairs, he decided to follow her, so he ran up after her. But when he got half way up, he saw that she was now coming down. She had also recognized him and had decided to follow him! When they at last caught each other, they talked excitedly about the old times in Germany and arranged to see each other again. A few years later, Drucker and Doris were married – it was a partnership that lasted for the rest of the century!

◆

While he was in London, Drucker thought very hard about the events in Germany. Why had the Nazis come to power? he asked himself. He decided that it was the result of changes in the societies and the economies of European countries. The modern world had brought big changes to the way that people lived. In Europe and America people had left the farms and the countryside and moved to the cities to find work in factories and offices. The old ideas of society didn't mean anything to these people any more. The problem was that there were no good new ideas to replace them. He felt that ordinary people had lost hope in the future. In Germany, the solution to this problem was Adolf Hitler and the Nazis. But Drucker was sure that this problem could be solved in other ways.

He put his ideas into a book called *The End of Economic Man*. It was published in 1939, just before the start of the Second World War. It was an immediate success among certain kinds of people. The British politician Winston Churchill (who had not yet become a war leader) read the book and said that it was excellent. He said that all top soldiers in the British army should receive a copy to help them to understand the international situation. Drucker later learnt that they received his book in a package that also contained the famous children's story *Alice In Wonderland*.

So, what did that say about the world's opinion of his ideas?

♦

At the end of the 1930s, Peter and Doris Drucker crossed the Atlantic and set up home in the USA. Drucker soon found a job as a teacher at Bennington College in Vermont. But he didn't stop thinking about the ideas in his first book. He decided that many of the problems of the modern world were problems that had been created by business. Business had lots of power in modern society, but it did not always use this power responsibly.

36

He thought that companies needed to think more carefully about their purpose and about their duty to look after their workers. But if business had caused the problems, then business could also solve them. In his next book, *The Future of Economic Man*, he said that the future of society was all about the future of organizations.

Drucker wanted to find out more about big business organizations. But as the world was at war, he knew he had to wait. Every big company in the USA was working as hard as possible to produce equipment for the army. Drucker realized that managers had no time to talk to a university teacher like him. Then, one day in 1943, he was sitting in his office at Bennington College, when he received a phone call.

'Hello, Mr Drucker,' said the voice. 'I'm calling from General Motors. We'd like to talk to you about something. Can you come for a meeting?'

Two days later Drucker visited General Motors' offices. There, he met one of the top managers, Donaldson Brown.

'We've read your books,' Brown told him, 'and people at GM are interested in your ideas. We're mostly technical and financial people here, but we're asking the same questions as you. What is the place of big business in society? How should a big organization be run? That sort of thing.'

Drucker couldn't believe his ears.

'Well, obviously I'm very happy to hear that,' he said. 'But how can I help you?'

'We have to start planning for the years after the war has finished,' Brown explained. 'So we'd like you to come to GM and look at our work. We'd like you to think about our organization and our methods and then write a report for top management.'

'That sounds very interesting,' said Drucker, 'but I already have a job at Bennington College.'

'That's OK,' said Brown. 'We don't want to employ you. We

want someone from outside. You can keep your job at Bennington, but of course, we'll pay you some extra money.'

For Drucker it was a great opportunity. General Motors was the most powerful company in the world. Drucker also wanted to meet GM's boss, Alfred Sloan. Sloan and his ideas were already famous in the business world. Drucker had heard that Sloan kept tight central control of the company's direction and its finances. But he also knew that Sloan allowed GM's managers to be independent and he liked to listen to their opinions.

When Drucker met him for the first time, he saw immediately that Sloan believed strongly in duty.

'Mr Drucker,' said Sloan, 'you have probably heard that I didn't want you to study General Motors. I saw no reason for your work. But my managers disagreed with me and so we took a decision to invite you here. This means that it is my duty to make sure that you do the best possible job. Come and see me at any time. Ask me any question you like. You can attend our meetings and you can make suggestions. I only ask that you do not tell people our secrets.'

Drucker admired Sloan but when he looked around the rest of GM, he was often surprised. On several occasions, he found a big difference between Sloan's ideas and the real world of GM's factories and offices.

One of Drucker's first appointments at GM was with a man called Marvin Coyle. Coyle was head of Chevrolet. He was a big man with hard, mean eyes. Many of Chevrolet's employees were afraid of him. Coyle knew it, but he was the kind of man who didn't care. One morning, Coyle was telling Drucker about the importance of Sloan's ideas.

'We like our managers to be independent,' said Coyle. 'We want them to take their own decisions.'

At that moment, the conversation was interrupted as a message started to come through on the noisy machine behind him.

'Is everything all right?' asked Drucker.

'Oh yes,' said Coyle. 'That's just the manager in Kansas City. He always tells me when he goes out to lunch.'

Drucker shook his head.

'So that's what "independent" means, is it?' he said to himself.

◆

Although GM had only asked Drucker to write a report, he soon realized that he had enough ideas for a book. Business books were not popular at that time, but he found a publisher and called it *Concept of the Corporation*. On the whole, the book was very positive about General Motors. Drucker was very enthusiastic about Sloan's way of mixing central control and independence for managers. But he also found a few faults. He was especially worried about the company's attitude towards its workers. At that time all businesses were tough on the workers. At General Motors they were only employed when there was a job to do. During the company's quiet times, many workers sat at home and earned nothing at all. When they were able to work, managers often shouted at them and ordered them to work harder.

But as early as the 1920s, people had asked if this was the right way to manage. An Australian called Elton Mayo had done some tests with 20,000 workers at Western Electric's Hawthorne factory outside Chicago. He wanted to see the effects of different lighting conditions on the factory's production. In the first test, the lighting conditions in the Hawthorne factory were improved. The result was that workers increased their production. In the second test, the lighting conditions were made worse. Perhaps surprisingly, production went up again. Finally, lighting conditions in the factory were returned to normal. And once again, the workers' production improved.

How could Elton Mayo explain these results? He decided that the improvements in production had nothing to do with the changes in lighting conditions. Production had only increased because the workers felt valued – and they felt valued simply because they were part of his test.

Elton Mayo said that this showed that it was important for managers to be good to workers. It was not enough for managers to offer extra money for good work and punishments for bad work. He said that people work harder when they feel their work is valued. Managers needed to understand that they were dealing with human beings and not machines.

Drucker thought in a similar way. In *Concept of the Corporation* he wrote that business should not see workers simply as a cost. The workers are the most important thing in any company. He believed that they should help to manage the company. He also said companies like GM should improve the workers' conditions and pay them regular money in good times and in bad.

Drucker thought that these points were completely fair, but when the top management of General Motors read the book, they were very angry.

'This is not a study of General Motors,' said Marvin Coyle, 'it is an attack on the company.'

Alfred Sloan wanted nothing to do with it.

Nearly all the people that Drucker had worked with at GM stopped speaking to him.

If any GM manager was found with a copy of the book, he was told, 'It's probably best if you go and work for Mr Ford.'

◆

While he was working at General Motors, Drucker often asked people, 'What books on management have you read?'

The answer was nearly always the same.

'There aren't any books on management, are there?'

Then one day, one of the GM managers suggested that he should visit a man called Harry Hopf.

'I'm told he's got the biggest collection of business books in the world,' he said.

A few days later, Drucker was knocking on the door of Harry Hopf's house in New York. An old man answered the door.

'So, young man,' said Hopf. 'I understand that you are interested in management.'

Hopf led him into a huge library that contained thousands and thousands of books. Drucker looked around him.

'Are all these books about management?' he asked.

Hopf laughed.

'No, young man,' he said. 'These are mostly about selling, advertising and production. I have, I believe, only six books about management in the whole library.'

In fact, when Drucker looked at Hopf's six management books more closely, he found that three of them weren't really about management at all. It was clear that if Drucker wanted to read any more books on management, he would have to write them himself.

In the years immediately after the Second World War, Drucker thought deeply about business and the job of a manager. In 1954, he published a book called *The Practice of Management*. According to some people, it was the book that invented management.

In the book, he asked some important questions. Probably the most important one was: what is a business? At that time, most people's answer was: an organization that tries to make a profit. But Drucker disagreed. For him, business wasn't just about money. He said that a business should always be a part of society. He said that business should always act responsibly. For him, the purpose of business is to create a customer. A business should always make something that people want to buy. It might be a completely new product, or it might be something that people have always wanted. But businesses should never try to trick people and business people should never be greedy. The purpose of business was to serve society. If business people got rich as a result, that was their fair reward.

And what about managers? What exactly was their job in Drucker's idea of business? To explain, Drucker told a simple story.

One day, he said, there were three workers who were all cutting some large pieces of stone. A stranger went up to them and asked, 'What are you men doing?'

The first man looked up from his work and said, 'I am earning some money.'

The second replied, 'I am doing the best job of stonecutting in the country.'

But the third man stopped and said, 'I am building a beautiful and enormous church.'

The third man, Drucker explained, was the true manager.

For Drucker, management wasn't just about the everyday running of a business. For him, a manager was someone who could see into the future. A manager was someone who could bring together people's skills and energies to produce something that was exciting and new. In the old world, the most important creative person had been the artist; in the modern world of organizations, according to Drucker, it was the manager.

But, in practice, how could a manager do this? Drucker's answer was 'management by objectives' (MBO). He said that a manager's job was not just to accept orders from above. A manager should always understand where he or she wants to go. A company should set an objective for a manager and then reward that person when they succeeded. Over the next twenty years MBO was accepted by almost every big company in the world.

◆

Since the 1950s, Drucker's ideas have become more and more important. As well as a university teacher, he has also been a consultant to businesses and governments. People have always been ready to listen to his ideas because it seems that Drucker is able to see the future very clearly. In 1959, most people in the world worked with their hands in factories or fields. Rich economies made their money from factories and physical strength. The most important products were things like planes, cars and trains. But 1959 was also the year that Drucker first talked about the knowledge worker. He said that more and more people are going to start working with their brains. He said that information and ideas will have a higher value than oil, wood and iron. Today, in many countries, the computer has made that situation a reality. But when Drucker first had those thoughts, the computer that sits on your desk today was the size of a small house!

In the 1960s, Drucker also thought hard about the job of government in society. He believed that the real purpose of government was to make decisions and to lead society. He was worried that many governments also tried to run businesses. He said that governments were bad at doing things themselves, because they nearly always wasted time and money. His solution was for governments to sell their businesses to private companies. In 1969, it seemed like a crazy idea. It was the time of the Cold War. In countries like China and the Soviet Union, governments owned all the businesses in the country. Even in places like Western Europe and the USA, governments owned many of their country's factories and services. It was almost impossible to believe that anything could change.

But some people were listening to Drucker, and during the 1970s his ideas spread from the world of business into the world of politics. In the early 1980s, the UK's new Prime Minister,

Margaret Thatcher tested Drucker's ideas about government for the first time.

Margaret Thatcher, tested Drucker's ideas about government for the first time. She started selling many of Britain's government businesses, like car factories and telephone companies, to the private part of the economy. Many people criticized Thatcher and said that she was selling things that belonged to the British people. But, soon governments in the rest of Europe and Latin America were copying Britain. And in the early 1990s, after the end of the Soviet Union, even Russia started to sell some of its factories and farms. Drucker had never dreamt that his ideas could travel so far!

◆

Peter Drucker has had a big effect not just on business, but also on the world beyond the factory and the office. But management has always been at the centre of his thinking. So what about Drucker's own ability as a manager? He has never really been a businessman himself. And, perhaps, that's a good thing. With complete honesty, Drucker once said, 'I would be a very poor manager. Hopeless. And a company job would be very, very boring.'

Chapter 4   The Management Superstar

Tom Peters

The man on the stage stops talking for a moment and takes off his jacket. He is so hot that everyone can see that his shirt is wet. 'Some people will tell you that they have all the answers,' he says. 'But not me. I know nothing. In this world we all know nothing. Zero. And do you know why? It's because the business world is changing too quickly.'

Some of the people who are watching look at each other and shake their heads.

'Look at General Motors. They knew it all. That's why they didn't prepare for the oil price increase in the 1970s. That's why they didn't notice the Japanese car industry. Oh yes, General Motors knew it all.'

A few people now start to laugh. So the man on the stage stops and points at them.

'Why are you laughing? General Motors was the biggest company in the world. It was probably a hundred times bigger than your company. And its managers were probably a hundred times better too. But their problem was that they thought they knew it all and, really, they knew nothing. And that is my message today.'

The people who are watching are all very successful businessmen and businesswomen. They have each paid over $1,000 for their seats. So why are they watching a man who knows nothing? Why do they listen to his insults?

The reason is that the man is Tom Peters – the star of the management world. He earns over $50,000 for each talk. Millions

Tom Peters

and millions of people have bought his books. The world's top companies ask his advice.

◆

Tom Peters would like you to believe that he's a little bit crazy. The serious Peter Drucker introduced the idea of management by objectives, an idea which was often called MBO. As an answer to Drucker, Peters suggested MBWA. And what did that mean? Management by walking around!

At his talks, Peters sometimes shows a painting in the style of Jackson Pollock. It looks like the artist has thrown a can of paint at the picture.

'The plan of your organization should look like this,' Peters tells his listeners. They shake their heads. What does he mean? But when they think about it more carefully, his ideas become clearer. He's trying to tell them that business isn't tidy and well ordered. Business is messy. Business is always changing. To succeed, the modern business person needs to think in new ways.

Some business people might think that Peters and his ideas are a joke. But behind his strange behaviour, Peters has always been a very serious person.

He was a young man in the 1960s. It was a time when many young Americans grew their hair long and sang songs about peace and love. But not Peters. He was a serious student and worked hard to pass his examinations in engineering at Cornell University. It was also the time of the Vietnam war. Many US students marched on the streets to show that they wanted their government to stop the fighting. But Peters didn't. He had an arrangement with the US army. They paid for his education and he agreed to work for them when he left university. As a result, his first job was as an engineer who built roads and bridges for US soldiers in Vietnam. After his time in Vietnam, Peters studied at Stanford, one of the USA's top business schools, and then got a job with the famous company of management consultants, McKinsey & Co.

McKinsey earns over $2 billion a year by selling advice to some of the biggest and most important companies in the world. A McKinsey report can cost several million dollars. It can do this because it employs the top people from the world's best business schools.

After leaving McKinsey, many of its consultants have become famous people in politics or business. Lou Gerstner, the head of IBM, worked for several years as a McKinsey consultant; Robert Haas, worked there before he became boss of Levi Strauss and Co. William Hague, the leader of the UK's Conservative party, also spent some time with the company.

When Tom Peters joined the San Francisco office of McKinsey in 1974, he was thirty-two years old and he had little real experience of the business world. He soon found that McKinsey was a tough place to work. Consultants must be ready to travel anywhere in the world at any time. They often have to work over a hundred hours a week. And if they fail, they are soon looking for another job. At McKinsey, it is not possible to stay at the same level for your whole working life. Either you are good enough to get a better job inside the company, or you are asked to leave.

McKinsey takes its name from the man who started the company, James O. McKinsey. But the person behind the company's great success was really Marvin Bower. Bower became the boss of the company in the 1930s. He wanted McKinsey to have an image like a law company or a bank. He said that his company's advice should always be expensive so that its customers took it seriously. He said that its consultants should never talk about its customers' business. He said that McKinsey's consultants should always dress in dark suits, ties and hats. And for some strange reason, he also told them always to wear long socks. Obviously, McKinsey's consultants were not chosen for their legs!

Peters's work at McKinsey gave him the chance to go round the world and to see businesses in many different countries. As he travelled, he became interested in the question: what makes an excellent company? More and more people wanted to hear his answer and soon McKinsey was asking him to give talks about his ideas to some of its biggest customers.

Then in July 1980, Peters had a meeting with Lew Jones, the boss of the US magazine, *Business Week*.

'We like your ideas,' said Jones. 'Can you write something for us?'

A week later, the front cover of *Business Week* said, 'Putting excellence into management.' Inside, there was a four-page piece by Tom Peters that explained his main ideas. Although it was on page 196 of the magazine, lots of people read it and liked it. Peters says, 'That was a huge piece of luck. The phone started ringing. It was the last day of peace I ever had.'

One of the phone calls was from a publishing company. They wanted him to write a book. Peters worked hard on the book for the rest of that year and continued into 1981. In fact, he found it very hard to stop and by late summer of that year he had written 1,300 pages. As a writer, Peters obviously had a lot to learn. The publishing company had asked him for a business book; they didn't want another *War and Peace*!

Peters asked for help from one of his colleagues at McKinsey, Robert Waterman. Waterman was very different to the noisy, energetic Peters. He was a quiet man who enjoyed painting and he had a very clear mind. Waterman agreed to rewrite Peters's book and to make it much shorter. By the spring of 1982, the work was finished. Now, they only needed a title.

Both Peters and Waterman wanted to call it 'The Secrets of Excellence'. They liked it, the publishing company liked it, in fact everybody liked it, except the boss of McKinsey, Marvin Bower. He called the two men to his office.

'As you know,' he said, 'McKinsey never tells anyone its customers' secrets. Gentlemen, I suggest that you find a new title.'

Peters said afterwards, 'It was like an order from God.'

Peters and Waterman thought hard about a new title. Peters suggested that they should call the book 'Management By Walking Around', but in the end he and Waterman decided on the title *In Search of Excellence*.

◆

When the book was published in October 1982, nobody expected it to be a great success. The publishing company only produced 15,000 copies. Some magazines wrote about it, but they were not very enthusiastic. Most people simply ignored it.

But *In Search of Excellence* was the right book at the right time. In the early 1980s, many Americans had lost confidence in their country's economy. The big increase in oil prices in the 1970s had had a bad effect on US business and by 1982 over 10 per cent of US workers were unemployed. Many people blamed US business for this situation. They said that Japanese companies were making products that were cheaper and better quality than US ones. They said that US business people had lost their way and that things were going downhill fast.

But Tom Peters and Robert Waterman disagreed. Their message was that Americans didn't need to worry too much about the Japanese competition. They said that there were many examples of excellent companies in the USA and in their book, they described forty-three of them. Nobody was very surprised by the companies they chose. They were nearly all big businesses like IBM, Proctor & Gamble, Johnson & Johnson and Exxon. But Peters and Waterman explained that these companies were successful because they did simple things well. These were companies that were close to their customers and that made things that the market really wanted. Above all, these were companies that didn't think of their workers as machines. They were companies that put people first.

It was exactly the message that Americans wanted. After a slow start, the book started to sell in huge quantities and passed a million in its first eleven months. By the end of 1985 around five million people had bought it.

But as Peters soon realized, the book's success wasn't just because of its message. *In Search of Excellence* had made business fashionable for the first time. People wanted a copy because it looked good on their bookshelves. Tom Peters guessed that although five million people had bought the book, only half of those people had opened it, perhaps 500,000 had read a few chapters and probably only 100,000 people had actually read it all.

Perhaps it was a good thing that so few people actually read it. Because, soon, people started to notice that the excellent companies in the book were not so excellent any more. Two years after it was published, a US business magazine showed that a quarter of the 'excellent' companies were having problems. Five years later two-thirds of the 'excellent' companies were in trouble and some had gone out of business completely!

But Tom Peters wasn't worried about that. He has never been afraid to say that he's wrong. And he's always been happy to change his mind. In fact, he started his 1987 book, *Thriving on Chaos*, with the words, 'There are no excellent companies.'

In the five years between *In Search of Excellence* and *Thriving on Chaos*, Peters travelled all over the world and gave thousands of talks to business people. During that time, his ideas about business changed. *In Search of Excellence* had accepted that in business, big was best. But in 1987, Peters thought that many businesses were too big. He believed that traditional companies suffered from too much central control and they employed too many people. In the past, the bosses of big companies had communicated with workers through middle managers. The job of a middle manager, said Peters, was really just to collect and control information. But that was now a job that could be done by a computer. Computers could allow ordinary workers to make more of their own decisions. If you were a middle manager in a large company, Peters was saying to you, 'It's time to find something else to do with your life!'

Once again, Peters found that his book was published at exactly the right time. The day it arrived in bookshops was 19 October 1987. In the financial world that day will always be remembered as Black Monday. On that day, billions and billions of dollars were lost as stock exchanges around the world fell by huge amounts. The message from the stock exchanges was clear: the world is a dangerous place. Peters's message in *Thriving on Chaos* was clear, too: this book will help you to deal with the problem.

◆

Events in the years after 1987 showed that many of Peters's ideas in *Thriving on Chaos* were quite right. The speed of change in the business world increased greatly. Big business hit big problems. Computers became more and more important. And thousands of middle managers lost their jobs as businesses tried to become smaller.

In the 1990s Tom Peters's ideas changed again. He said that managers needed to prepare for the changes of the modern world in new ways. Business was changing faster than ever before and he believed that traditional companies needed to learn lessons from the worlds of fashion, films, TV and computers.

He said that companies should be ready to change every day of the year. He told them they needed to be more like the US TV company, CNN. In the newsroom at CNN, careful planning was impossible. Every day, anything could happen. A war could start, a president could die, there could be a huge natural disaster. Just like CNN, said Tom Peters, every company needs to invent itself again every day.

He told businesses that they should be more like the companies of Silicon Valley, the area just south of San Francisco in California. Silicon Valley is the home of the world's computer industry. It's a place where people can make a billion dollars before they're thirty. But it's also a place where many people fail. But in Silicon Valley, nobody's worried about that. They accept that you only learn to be a success by making plenty of mistakes.

He also admired Silicon Valley's attitude to work. There, nobody expects a job for life. Companies come and go all the time and people are happy to move from job to job. They say that if you decide to change your job on the way to work in the morning, you just drive your car into a different company's car park! So, in the future, will that be the situation for everybody in every industry?

Tom Peters would confidently answer, 'Yes'.

◆

Tom Peters is a hard man to describe. He's probably the world's most famous management guru and yet he says, 'I attack managers for a living.'

He is a serious writer and thinker but he has appeared on one of his book covers without his trousers on.

He gives talks to some of the richest and most powerful bosses in the world and tells them, 'Workers in the United States and England have been used like dog food for the past 150 years.'

So how do you really get to the heart of his ideas? As always, Tom Peters says it best himself, 'Crazy times call for crazy people.'

Chapter 5   The Best of the Rest

Rosabeth Moss Kanter and Charles Handy

Since the success of Tom Peters, many new management thinkers have tried to become gurus. There are gurus who compare business with sport, there are gurus who say that business should learn the lessons of religion and, of course, there are gurus who simply state the obvious.

The truth is that the business world is now so competitive that companies are ready to pay huge amounts of money for almost any new ideas. As a result, it's sometimes hard to tell the difference between a real management guru and someone who just wants to get rich quickly.

But as well as Taylor, Sloan, Drucker and Peters, there are two other management thinkers who are certainly great modern gurus – Rosabeth Moss Kanter and Charles Handy.

♦

Rosabeth Moss Kanter is one of the very few women management gurus. She has spent her working life studying the problems of large companies and the ways they have to change to compete in the modern world. She believes that large companies today are in a kind of Olympic Games for business. She says that just like the Olympics, business is now an international competition. And just like the Olympics, modern business tests the skill and strength of people who work on their own and people who work in teams. But, of course, the big difference between business and the real Olympics is the kind of games that are played.

According to Kanter, companies now find that they are playing games like the one in the children's story *Alice In*

Wonderland. In the *Alice In Wonderland* game, the equipment is always different from one moment to the next. In modern business, she says, it's exactly the same situation. In *Alice In Wonderland*, the rules of the game are always changing. In modern business, it's the same thing again; nobody knows what will happen next. And in *Alice In Wonderland*, the game is often interrupted by a mad Queen who shouts, 'Off with his head!', for no good reason. So what's the comparison here? Well, most business people would probably agree that their plans are too often destroyed by strange people for no good reason at all! So how can companies succeed in this kind of game? Kanter says that they need to have the size and strength of the old big businesses, but they also need to be as quick and inventive as a modern small business.

Kanter says that if big businesses want to continue to be successful, then they must learn to dance.

◆

Charles Handy is an Irishman who shares Rosabeth Moss Kanter's interest in the idea of change. Handy had a successful working life with the oil company, Shell, before he became a management writer and a teacher at business schools. But Handy has also always been interested in religion. His father was a religious leader in Ireland and at one time he too thought of joining the church. Perhaps as a result, his thinking always has a strong sense of right and wrong.

Handy believes that we are living in a time of huge change. In one of his books, he compares our situation to the situation of the people who lived in South America around five hundred years ago. He tells a story about a South American person who once looked out to sea and saw a large sailing ship. This person had never seen a sailing ship like this before, so he decided that it couldn't exist.

Charles Handy

'There's nothing to worry about,' he told himself. 'It's just a strange effect of the weather.'

The ship existed, of course, and it was full of Spanish soldiers. When they landed on the coast of South America, they changed the lives of the people there for ever.

Handy thinks that when we look into the distance, we too can see the shape of our future lives. But, just like the South American in his story, we choose to put those thoughts out of our mind. He thinks that this is a big mistake. He says we should be worried about the things that we can see in the distance. We should be worried because the things in the distance are frightening. We should be worried because these things will change our lives in big ways. And we should be worried because we aren't ready for those changes.

In the past, he says that we lived in an age of reason. There was order in the world and everything was organized. People understood the changes that happened, even if they didn't always accept them. But today we live in an age of unreason. In the age of unreason nobody really understands what's happening in the modern world and nobody can really explain it.

So how can we deal with these changes? Handy tells us to forget about our old ideas. To understand the modern world, he says we need 'upside down' thinking. We have to imagine the impossible and expect the unexpected. And how can we do this? We can do this by using the three 'I's: information, ideas and intelligence.

Just like Peter Drucker and Tom Peters, Handy believes that knowledge workers and computers are changing the business world. He says that in future, company life and office life will start to disappear. More and more people will become independent and will work for themselves. They'll work from home and use the telephone and the computer to communicate with other people. This should be good news for companies, because they

58

won't need to have so many expensive office buildings in the middle of cities and they won't need to pay so many people regular money. But how does this affect ordinary workers?

Charles Handy hopes that their lives will improve. He believes that in the future people will have more time for their family and friends, because they won't have to travel to work every day and will often work from home. But in other ways, their lives will become more difficult. Most people will probably need more than one job and more than one skill to make a living. Perhaps teachers will also need to be writers and consultants. Perhaps policemen will have to be guards and private detectives.

But when the world is turned upside down, who knows what will happen?

◆

The thinking of management gurus has come a long way since the time of Frederick Taylor and scientific management. For Taylor, management was certainly not about crazy people or company Olympics or upside down thinking.

But, although management gurus have produced all sorts of very different ideas, in the end, how useful are they for real businessmen and businesswomen?

Many people have criticized the management gurus. Many have said that their ideas are a waste of time. But before anyone forgets their ideas completely, perhaps they should remember the story of some Hungarian soldiers who were lost in the Alps.

The Hungarian soldiers had got lost on a freezing night and had almost no food. Their situation was very serious and they didn't know what to do. Then, one of the soldiers reached into his pocket and took out a map. The soldiers studied the map for a long time and discussed the best route. After a long and difficult walk, they were able to come down from the mountains and they found a village with some food and a roof for the night.

The interesting thing about the story is that the soldier's map was a map of a completely different area of the Alps. It had given them no useful information at all. But that map had been enough to make them think and to make them talk about their problem. And that's what saved their lives.

ACTIVITIES

Chapter 1

Before you read

1 Frederick Taylor is famous for 'scientific management'. What do you know about it? What do you guess that it's about?

2 Find the words in *italics* in your dictionary. Match each word with a word below. What is the connection?

   create   huge   replace   tough   ton   wind(wound)   worth

   a make   **b** big   **c** watch   **d** value
   e weight   **f** change   **g** strong

3 Find these words in your dictionary.

   steel works   investment company   manufacturing

   Which are words for

   a making all sorts of things?
   b making money?
   c making a kind of metal?

After you read

4 What kind of family did Taylor come from?
5 Why did he take a job as an ordinary worker?
6 What was his sporting success?
7 What did he teach Schmidt at Bethlehem?
8 How did he become famous?
9 Can you think of ways in which Taylor's ideas still affect our lives today?

Chapter 2

Before you read

10 What do you think makes a good company man or a good company woman? What qualities and attitudes do you think that person should have?

11 Find these words in your dictionary.

   automobile   downmarket   upmarket   finances   hearing aid
   leadership   pressure   united

Which words mean

a together?

b cheap and low quality?

c expensive and high quality?

d car?

e a machine to help you hear?

f money?

g force or urgency?

h the qualities of a boss?

After you read

12 What was General Motors' situation when Sloan became its boss?

13 How did Sloan and Dreystadt solve Cadillac's problems in the 1930s?

14 What was Sloan's attitude to workers?

15 Why did Sloan help Henry Ford II?

16 Why did GM cars look so strange in the 1950s?

17 What are the good points and the bad points about Sloan's ideas of management?

Chapter 3

Before you read

18 Drucker says that the purpose of business is 'to create a customer'. What other purpose could business have?

19 Answer these questions. Find the words in *italics* in your dictionary.

a What is a *technical* fault?

b What kind of things do you *publish*?

c What's an example of a *partnership*?

d What kind of person has *objectives*?

e What word has a similar meaning to *obvious*?

f What's the opposite of 'to tell the *truth*'?

After you read

20 Why did Drucker leave Germany?

21 Why did he want to study General Motors?

22 What faults did he find at that company?

23 What's the meaning of the story of the stonecutters?

24 Which of Drucker's ideas did Mrs Thatcher borrow?

Chapter 4

Before you read

25 What do you already know about Tom Peters? What kind of person is he?

26 Answer these questions. Find the words in *italics* in your dictionary.

    a What kind of person has a tough *image*?

    b What do you think a management *consultant* does?

    c How many *superstars* can you name?

    d When you *ignore* someone, what do you do?

After you read

27 What did Peters do when he was young?

28 What kind of company is McKinsey?

29 Why was Peters's first book so successful?

30 What is the future like for middle managers in big companies?

31 What ideas should big business copy from Silicon Valley?

32 Do you think that it's important for people to have a serious attitude to management?

Chapter 5

Before you read

33 What do you think are the three main problems facing modern business?

After you read

34 In what ways is business like a company Olympics?

35 What does Kanter say that big companies need to learn to do?

36 Why should we remember the story of the South American and the sailing ship today?

37 In what way are changes in the modern world good for companies?

38 What's the connection between the management gurus and the Hungarian soldiers lost in the Alps?

39 How many other management gurus do you know? What ideas are they famous for?

Writing

40 Write a short e-mail to a colleague that gives a one or two line description of each of the gurus in the book.

41 Write a short report. Suggest to a friend or colleague that he or she reads the ideas of one of the gurus in the book. Your report should talk about the strong points of this guru's ideas and the weak points of the others.

42 Imagine that Frederick Taylor became the boss of your company, university or school. Write a list of the changes that he would make.

43 Tell Peter Drucker's story of the stonecutters in your own words and then explain its connection with management.

44 Write a newspaper article about three ways in which you think that business life will change over the next twenty years. Explain why you think this.

45 Imagine that you have to write an advertisement for one of Tom Peters's talks. What would you say about him?